RAF TANGMERE
REVISITED

THE LONG FAREWELL

TANGMERE is closing down, they say;
They've dined the Squadrons out and soon
The wise face of the Hunters' moon
Will see them scattered far away.

THE old pens where the fighters lay
Awaiting the marauding Hun
Lie empty now, like ancient scars
Weed-grown beneath the setting sun.

THE Squadrons climb against the sky,
Deep-etched against the dying light,
The wind stirs softly, like a sigh
For those who fly and those who fight.

THIS field, as famed as Agincourt,
Or Crécy, with their mailed hosts,
Where those who valued freedom fought,
Sleeps, guarded by its valiant ghosts.

Hannah M. Hunt

RAF Tangmere Revisited

Revisited

ANDY SAUNDERS

SUTTON PUBLISHING LIMITED

Sutton Publishing Limited
Phoenix Mill · Thrupp · Stroud
Gloucestershire · GL5 2BU

First published 1998

British Library Cataloguing in Publication Data
A catalogue record for this book is available from the
British Library.

ISBN 0-7509-1906-X

Typeset in 10/12 Perpetua.
Typesetting and origination by
Sutton Publishing Limited.
Printed in Great Britain by
Ebenezer Baylis, Worcester.

*For my children Jonathan, Steven, Clare & Katherine.
Also, for old friends who created Tangmere Military Aviation
Museum and built what it became.*

CONTENTS

INTRODUCTION

The Royal Air Force Station at Tangmere was one of the most famous in the history of the Service; it was also one of the finest. This book serves as a photographic record of this historic airfield, an airfield of which one famous pilot wrote: 'During my twenty years' service with RAF Fighter Command I served at every major station, a number of which looked like gypsy encampments. I can mention Biggin Hill, Kenley, West Malling, Hawkinge, Manston, Gravesend, Hornchurch, North Weald, Duxford, Coltishall – even Exeter, to make the point. But there never was, and never will be, a station so attractive as Tangmere. Even the poetry of the name gives it away.' Its origins, however, can be traced to an otherwise insignificant forced landing by an FE26 aeroplane during the First World War.

On 19 November 1916 Lt Geoffrey Dorman of the Royal Flying Corps was en route from Shoreham to Gosport when engine problems forced him to make an emergency landing in a field. That field was at George Bayley's Church Farm, Tangmere, and Dorman, realizing that the site would make an excellent aerodrome, reported on the fact to the War Office. The result was that construction work began in 1917 for a permanent air station at Tangmere and in March 1918, 91, 92 and 93 Squadrons of the RFC moved in before transferring across the Channel to France. It was further intended that the United States Army Air Force would use Tangmere as a training depot for its Handley Page O/400 aeroplanes, but the Armistice came shortly after the Americans moved in. Consequently the station became redundant and was handed back to the newly formed RAF but closed down in December 1919.

In 1925 the station was reopened to accommodate a coastal storage unit of the Fleet Air Arm, but Tangmere's history as an operational RAF station dates from the formation of a station headquarters in November 1926 and the arrival some days later of 43 Squadron, equipped at the time with Gloster Gamecocks. Early the next year, 1 Squadron moved in with its Siskin fighters and so began a long association between Tangmere and the two squadrons, with their intense rivalry to excel in all aspects of flying. In 1930, at the annual Hendon Air Pageant, 43 Squadron staggered the crowd with a breathtaking exhibition of aerobatics. Flying a succession of loops, three flights of three aircraft each flew in formation linked together by cotton streamers.

In that period of the history of RAF Tangmere the station was a much sought-after posting with work concentrated into the morning during summer months, leaving the rest of the day clear for relaxation or sport. RAF Tangmere excelled at all kinds of sporting activity, particularly team games, but in athletics produced a champion hurdler, LAC D. Finlay, who went on to gain an Olympic medal.

Without a doubt the 1920s and 1930s were Tangmere's halcyon days and the silver biplanes with their colourful squadron markings epitomized the era. Sadly, however, by the mid-1930s these carefree days were numbered as the clouds of war loomed larger than ever before in Europe. Consequently, the importance of Tangmere in the UK's air defence system became even more significant than had hitherto been the case and in 1937, 72 Squadron was formed there with its Gloster Gladiator fighters, and 217 Squadron was posted in for reconnaissance duties with its Avro Anson aircraft.

By the summer of 1939 it was apparent to everyone that war was just around the corner and in August the ground defences at Tangmere were strengthened with the erection of barbed wire, gun emplacements and slit trenches. Meanwhile, as if the activities at Tangmere were no more important than the local confectioner's shop, the *Kelly's Directory* for that year listed the 'commercial' occupants of Tangmere as:

Jas. Northgate	Tangmere Hotel
Chas. J. Mansley	The Cosy Tea Rooms
A.S. Price & Sons	Dairymen, The Glebe
R.A.F. Station	1 & 43 Squadrons
R. Willard & Sons	Wheelwrights, carpenters and undertakers

On 3 September 1939 war with Germany was finally declared and a pilot of 1 Squadron (by now flying Hurricanes) wrote of that day: 'The sun shone just the same. The windmill on the hill looked just the same. The fields and woods and country lanes were the same. But we are at war.' That war was to change the face of Tangmere forever, and to earn the station a place in the history books.

On 8 September 1939, 1 Squadron flew out of Tangmere to take up war stations in France where the pilots' skill in battle reflected their prowess in peacetime. During the Battle of France, all squadrons and replacement aeroplanes were funnelled through Tangmere on their way to France; with the fall of France, Tangmere saw the flow in reverse as survivors trickled back into England.

As the Battle of Britain got into its stride during the summer of 1940 the Tangmere fighter squadrons were at the forefront of the action, their pre-war numbers swelled by the activation of a satellite landing ground at Westhampnett (now Goodwood Airport). Here were based 602 Squadron (Spitfires) and 145 Squadron (Hurricanes), while Tangmere itself saw the arrival of several Hurricane squadrons, including nos 1, 17, 43, 145, 213, 601 and 607, during that hectic and hard-fought summer.

Realizing its importance as an RAF sector station the Luftwaffe attempted to knock the airfield out of action in a devastating raid by Stuka dive-bombers on 16 August 1940. Damage was considerable: one hanger was burnt out and two wrecked beyond repair, while workshops, the armoury, sick quarters, central stores, officers' and sergeants' messes were all hit and damaged. Three Blenheims and seven Hurricanes were destroyed on the ground and at least forty vehicles lost; thirteen people were killed and another twenty seriously injured. Nevertheless, the Tangmere squadrons gave the attackers a severely bloodied nose and brought down several of the raiders nearby. Despite the damage and mayhem, the aerodrome remained operational.

With the Battle of Britain won, the tempo of the air war changed and the emphasis swung from defence to offence. A 'wing' of three Spitfire squadrons moved in during 1941, led by the legendary legless fighter pilot, Wg Cdr Douglas Bader, although in August of that year he was brought down over France and made a prisoner of war.

A period of expansion at Tangmere saw the opening of further satellite landing grounds at Merston, Appledram, Bognor, Funtington and Selsey. As with Westhampnett, all came under Tangmere's control.

The offensive nature of the air operations from Tangmere continued into 1942. On 12 February, 41 and 129 Squadrons took off in very bad weather to participate in the actions against the German warships *Scharnhorst*, *Gneisenau* and *Prinz Eugen* during their epic 'Channel Dash'; the pilots claimed three Me 109s destroyed and two damaged for the loss of two aircraft and pilots. Later that year, on 19 August, the Tangmere squadrons took part in the air battles over the Dieppe beaches in what was then the greatest single air battle of all time. Also in 1942 the Lysanders of 161 (Special Duties) Squadron began their clandestine night time operations from Tangmere, ferrying agents into and out of occupied France. The squadron, its operations cloaked in the greatest of secrecy, used Tangmere Cottage opposite the main gate of the station as its headquarters. Tangmere's proudest moment was probably the pivotal role it played during the achievement of air supremacy over the Normandy beaches on D-Day, 6 June 1944. The role of Tangmere's squadrons in the success of the D-Day operation cannot be over-estimated; since 1925 the station had won a reputation for the highest achievement in peace and war, and if 1940 had seen its finest hour then 1944 had surely seen its proudest.

As the fighting moved away across Europe the significance of RAF Tangmere diminished. After all the excitement and drama of the past months and years, 1945 was something of an anti-climax and with VE-Day and general demobilization the station's future seemed uncertain. However, at the war's end a tally of over 800 enemy aircraft destroyed, 245 probably destroyed and 432 damaged had been achieved by Tangmere-based squadrons. By any standards it was an impressive score, but how many pilots and how many aeroplanes it had cost is impossible to measure. Some indication of the cost in human terms may be seen in the churchyard of St Andrew's, Tangmere, with its rows of war graves, British and German.

After the war, the dawning of the jet age saw Meteors and then Hunter fighters based at Tangmere and the return, among others, of 1 and 43 Squadrons and the continuation of their traditional rivalries. In 1946 Gp Capt. F.M. 'Teddy' Donaldson broke the World Air Speed Record from Tangmere, in a Meteor jet fighter; this was followed by the smashing of the record by a Hawker Hunter flown by Sqn Ldr Neville Duke in 1953, again from Tangmere. Both aircraft were preserved and are now displayed at the Tangmere Military Aviation Museum.

By 1958 Tangmere's role as a fighter station had come to an end and it became a Signals Command station, housing Canberra and Varsity aircraft on signals calibration duties. In 1963, however, the flying squadrons moved out and the once proud station was relegated to use by 38 Group Support Unit, which included Naval and Army personnel, while the aerodrome itself was used by C-130 Hercules transport aircraft from nearby RAF Thorney Island for practising low-level supply drops. In the late 1960s a Defence Review concluded that RAF Tangmere had outlived its usefulness and, sadly, on a bleak and cold 20 October 1970, the RAF ensign was hauled down for the last time as a solitary Spitfire flew overhead in salute to the station and its valiant past. For a while, into the mid-1970s, a minor RAF presence in the form of No. 623 Gliding School remained on site. Thereafter for several years the Property Services Agency allowed the buildings to fall into decay and ruin until the aerodrome and its buildings, apart from the hangars and control tower, were sold for development and a new housing estate and business park now sprawl across what was once the finest fighter station in the history of the Royal Air Force. New roads also cut through the estate, but none of them was named to reflect the site's historic past. In 1980, however, the Tangmere Memorial Museum Company was founded and in 1982 set up a new air museum on the old aerodrome to honour the special place which Tangmere holds in British aviation history. This book is the author's second offering of a photographic record of Royal Air Force Station Tangmere and it is hoped it will offer readers a taste of Tangmere's former glory.

Andy Saunders
1998

CHAPTER ONE

RAF TANGMERE: THE EARLY YEARS

This aerial view of Tangmere, looking west, shows to advantage the layout of the station during the 1920s. Compare this picture with a similar view taken in 1980 on page 134.

GEOFFREY DORMAN,
A.R.Ae.S.
Air Correspondent.

Telephone : Mayfair 2901

30, Redburn Street,

London, S.W.3.

F.

P E

-9 FEB 1949

REF. No. 445/1.1

The Officer Commanding
R.A.F.Station,
Tangmere, Sussex.

8.2.49.

Dear Sir,
In October or November 1916 I was flying an F.E.2b from
Shoreham to Gosport. A quick sea fog formed, and as my motor was
misbehaving I decided it would be best to try and land. I came
down through the fog, cleared a row of trees and touched down. I
expected to hit something at any moment but stopped safely. When
the fog cleared I found I was in a huge field nearly as big as an
aerodrome. When I tried to take off, a large lump of clay was
thrown up into the propeller and broke a piece off the leading
edge, so I had to get another prop from Gosport before I could fly
back.
When I returned I made a report on this huge field which was
eventually made into Tangmere aerodrome.
I still have that prop and if you would like me to give it an
honoured resting place, I will be glad to let you have it.

For the last few years it has been at Kenley Air Station as I
lent it to an ATC Squadron stationed there. At the moment it is at
the Royal Aero Club Aviation Centre at Londonderry House as I am
having it there for the R.F.C.Reunion on March 31, which I have
organised. But after that.I think you can have it if you would
like it for your Mess. It is quite an ancient relic now

Yours sincerely

Lt Geoffrey Dorman's unintentional landing at Bayley's Farm, Tangmere, on 19 November 1916 had far-reaching consequences for the history of this tiny Sussex village and the Royal Air Force. This letter from Geoffrey Dorman offered the broken prop from his aeroplane to the officers' mess at Tangmere, where it hung until the station closed in 1970. Where is this historic relic today?

Eric Robbins
1983.

Shortly after Dorman's unscheduled landing at Tangmere another RFC pilot, Eric Robbins, also had to make an emergency landing at Tangmere after the engine in his Avro 504 failed. In 1983 Mr Robbins returned to the spot where he had landed almost seventy years earlier.

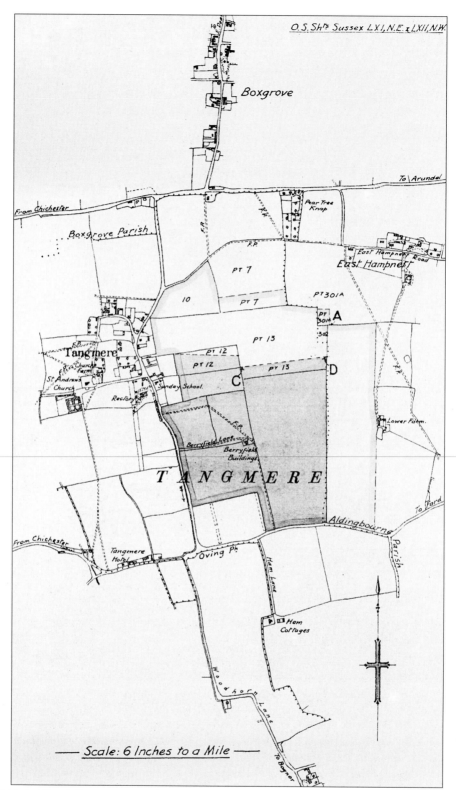

In 1923 the War Office requisitioned the site from Tangmere farmer George Bayley. This site plan of Tangmere was supplied to Mr Bayley to indicate how much land they wanted for the new aerodrome. Other drawings noted depressions to be infilled, trees to be felled and telegraph lines removed. RAF Tangmere re-opened in 1925.

CHAPTER TWO

ROARING TWENTIES, GLORIOUS THIRTIES

This evocative shot of Hawker Furies of 43 Squadron, airborne from Tangmere in the 1930s, epitomizes the period: silver-doped biplanes and colourful squadron markings. This peaceful and pastoral scene belied the purpose for which the Tangmere fighter squadrons trained and the fact that war clouds were already gathering in Europe. All too soon the leisurely formations and colourful machines would be a thing of the past – not to return to Tangmere's squadrons until the postwar era. The sight and sound, however, of silver biplane fighters became very familiar to the people of Sussex from Rye to Selsey Bill.

An SE5a, a civilianized ex-RAF fighter, visited Tangmere on 16 July 1921 during the first Oxford v. Cambridge air race. The winning Cambridge team pictured here (from left to right) was Mr Philcox, Mr Muir and Mr Francis.

In November 1926, 43 Squadron, led by Sqn Ldr A.F. Brooks, moved in with Gloster Gamecock fighters. The black and white chequerboards were the squadron markings.

This ungainly beast was an Avro 55A Bison II, N9851, and was one of only eighteen of the type ordered for the RAF in 1924. It is pictured during a visit to Tangmere in the spring of 1926. The huge bulk of its fuselage dwarfs the airman standing alongside.

This is a Hawker Horsley bomber, J8024, pictured inside one of the Belfast hangars at Tangmere, May 1930. The type had been in service with the RAF from 1926. Forty examples of this less-than-attractive aeroplane were built and, as with any unusual visitor to Tangmere, this one attracted a photographer or two!

In 1928, 43 Squadron re-equipped with the Armstrong Whitworth Siskin. This is one of the squadron machines with a Belfast hangar in the background. This aircraft sports the chequerboard markings but 43 Squadron's badge was a cockerel, earning the unit its nickname of 'The Fighting Cocks'.

Another Siskin but this one belonged to 1 Squadron. It is pictured with its groundcrew inside one of the Belfast hangars; note the wooden lattice roof trusses. On the left of the group is D.O. Finlay, a famous 1936 Olympic hurdler and later a notable Battle of Britain pilot.

The officers and men of 43 Squadron pose in front of the NAAFI building at Tangmere, 1929. Note the puttee leggings and the officers' walking sticks, which seem to be standard equipment. One of the few original buildings to survive on the original aerodrome site, it has now been converted into flats.

Sporting activities were always encouraged at RAF Tangmere and these were the winners of the West Sussex Senior Football League of 1929/30. The rather splendid trophy almost seems to outdo even the FA Cup! The officers still have their sticks but their puttees have been replaced by ordinary trousers.

More sporting prowess at Tangmere! This splendid photograph of 1932 commemorates the cricket match between the Tangmere Sergeants and the Black Dog and Duck at Bury, West Sussex. The portly gentleman seated in the centre is presumably the landlord of the Black Dog and Duck and captain of his team. We cannot identify which team is which or who were the winners, but as approximately half of the faces seem cheerful and the other half glum we can perhaps distinguish winners from losers! No doubt a few pints of ale would have cheered the losers. Perhaps the gentlemen wearing ties are the umpire and scorer, and the little boy must be one of the team mascots. The dog, although not black, presumably belongs to the pub landlord. Typical of the period are the striped blazers, sports jackets, open shirt collars, flat caps and co-respondent shoes.

This cartoon was drawn by an auxiliary Air Force Airman LAC E. Wren of 604 Squadron during summer camp at Tangmere. 'Chris' Wren became a famous aviation cartoonist and these early sketches were both clever and well executed. Particularly amusing is the comment about the unfortunate Walter Winchell Ablitt who 'knows less about more things than anybody I ever met'.

Landing mishaps were not uncommon and it was said that a good landing was one you could walk away from. This 1 Squadron Siskin, J9887, did a neat pirouette on the flying field in the summer of 1929. While this pilot walked away unhurt, the trek back to the flight hut must have seemed a long one as he worked out what to tell his CO!

Crunch! Another Siskin, this time of 43 Squadron, becomes a candidate for the repair shop. Airframe riggers and engine fitters were kept busy straightening bent aeroplanes or stripping useful spares from complete write-offs.

This Bristol fighter lost its undercarriage in a heavy landing at Tangmere during 1927. This was not a Tangmere-based machine and its history is unknown, although its squadron markings are a blue strip across the upper mainplane. Bristol fighters were a First World War type, but remained in service well into the 1920s.

Another mishap to a 1 Squadron Siskin, c. 1929. J9903 has suffered major damage to wings, undercarriage, tail and propeller but is probably not beyond repair.

This D.H. Moth of the Ferranti company was a visitor to Tangmere in about 1935 but the purpose of its stop is uncertain. The aeroplane may have been involved in some form of technical development for Ferranti.

Visiting aircraft at Tangmere for Empire Air Day, 1937. The types include a Handley Page Heyford, Gloster Gladiator, Hawker Hart and Westland Wallace. These air shows attracted huge crowds and were a thrilling spectacle for a very air-minded public.

This sleek Fairey II fighter visited Tangmere in about 1934. This was a pre-production machine. The type never went into production for the home market, although a number were delivered to foreign air forces.

This is the same aeroplane, pictured after coming to grief in a take-off accident at Tangmere. The aeroplane was dismantled and taken back to the Fairey works for repair.

Pilots of 43 Squadron relax off duty in the officers' mess at Tangmere, 1937. This once opulent building fell into ruin after the station closed in 1970 and, sadly, was eventually demolished. Just visible on the mantleshelf is an RAF clock which may now be seen in the entrance foyer to 10 Downing Street!

Hawker Furies of 43 Squadron, 'The Fighting Cocks', Tangmere 1937. The era of the biplane fighter was drawing to a close and one of the new Hawker Hurricane fighters can be seen in this picture. This was a visitor to Tangmere, although the squadrons there would soon be re-equipped with the type.

This Hawker Fury K2039 of 1 Squadron crashed at Tangmere in 1938 after hitting a ground target and damaging its undercarriage. The pilot was shaken but unhurt.

Hawker Fury K1939 of 43 Squadron looks rather the worse for wear after a landing accident at Tangmere, also in 1938. The Squadron's 'Fighting Cock' emblem can clearly be seen on the tail.

On 26 May 1932 two Hawker Fury aircraft of 1 Squadron collided during formation practice near Shoreham and crashed near Erringham Farm. Flg Off. Chatterton escaped by parachute from K2036.

The other aircraft, K2064, smashed into the ground, killing the twenty-year-old pilot, P/O Howard Jackson from Rhodesia. Another pilot in the flight, Flt Lt Anstruther, landed on Mill Hill, Shoreham, and helped to extract his colleague's body from the crumpled wreckage.

Avro Ansons of 217 Squadron, Coastal Command, moved into Tangmere as war clouds loomed during the late 1930s. They provided coastal and channel patrols on a round-the-clock basis.

This Anson over-shot the runway and ended up across the A27 road north of the village. It is hard to believe that this country lane is now the roaring dual carriageway between Brighton and Southampton!

CHAPTER THREE

PRELUDE TO WAR

On the day war broke out, 3 September 1939, a 43 Squadron groundcrewman struggles to work in his gas mask and gas cape. From the moment war was declared there was an expectation of imminent attack; air raid sirens sounded and gas masks were donned. Very soon, however, the Tangmere fighter squadrons were off to war on the continent where they acquitted themselves well in the Battle of France before returning to Tangmere at the time of the Dunkirk evacuation. During the 'Phoney War' of 1939 and early 1940, however, Tangmere saw a vast movement of men and machines through the aerodrome and regular changes to resident squadrons. A sense of expectation prevailed during this period of waiting but, very soon, the storm would well and truly break over RAF Tangmere. The station and its squadrons would not be found wanting!

The winter of 1939/40 was a severe one. Here, a 43 Squadron Hurricane, protected in its sand-bagged emplacement and sheeted in protective canvas, stands helplessly in drifting snow. Flying was impossible because of the weather, and attempts to clear runways of snow proved futile. But at least the Germans were grounded too!

Bristol Blenheim fighters of 601 Squadron at Tangmere during the same winter. This was an Auxiliary unit which became known as the 'Millionaires Squadron' because of the class of its members! Later, 601 Squadron would re-equip with Hawker Hurricanes.

The same winter, the same snow! The Silver Ansons of 217 Squadron were now in their drab war paint but Tangmere's Belfast hangars were still in their peacetime white finish. Statistically, this young airman, aged about twenty, stood little chance of surviving the long war ahead of him.

Looking more like troops from the Western Front in the First World War, this motley gang are in fact the 1 Squadron armourers, based at Headhone Farm, Lidsey. Note the interesting variety of working clothes and uniforms.

43 Squadron groundcrew pictured at Tangmere in 1939 with an aircraft refuelling bowser. Note the civilian tractor driver. Civilians were important employees on the station throughout its history. Seated fourth from left on the bowser is the late Jimmy Beedle, co-founder, with the author of this book, of Tangmere Museum.

Sgt Pilot Jack Ramshaw is pictured by a Hurricane of 1 Squadron, although he never served with them and presumably was just visiting Tangmere. He was shot down and killed on 4 September 1940 during the Battle of Britain, flying a Spitfire of 222 Squadron. Note the white lines on the hangar, shortly to be painted with a brown and green camouflage pattern.

Hurricanes of 43 Squadron fly low over the eastern boundary of Tangmere for a formation landing. Scrambles and patrols were the order of the day.

The Hurricanes of 501 Squadron were stationed at Tangmere from November 1939 to May 1940 when the squadron moved to Betheniville, France. In this photograph the aircraft are lined up on the concrete apron by the hangars. After the Battle of France 501 became the longest-serving squadron in the Battle of Britain, but did not return to Tangmere.

'They also served.' This is a WAAF driver of 501 Squadron with her Bedford truck at Tangmere in 1940. These women drivers often conveyed pilots to and from their messes and the aircraft dispersal points. Although relationships between WAAFs and pilots were frowned upon, some inevitably bloomed and flourished.

Three pilots of 43 Squadron wearing the standard flying headgear: helmet and headphones, oxygen mask with microphone, and flying goggles. Abandoning an aeroplane could be hazardous with the risk of entanglement in the leads and hoses, especially given that the pilot had only seconds in which to open the hood, undo the straps and get clear of both headgear and aircraft.

Pilots of 1 Squadron, pictured in France with a trophy liberated from a shot-down Messerschmitt Bf 110. The 'Flying One' badge carried the motto 'First in All Things', and the pilots of 1 Squadron were the first to shoot down a German aeroplane in France.

This is Sgt McKay, airborne from Tangmere in his 501 Squadron Hurricane, April 1940. On 18 August 1940, the hardest-fought day of the Battle of Britain, McKay's Hurricane was shot down near Whitstable but he parachuted to safety.

By 1939 the era of silver-doped fighters had gone and the new camouflaged Hurricane fighters were in service with 1 and 43 Squadrons at Tangmere. Here, a 1 Squadron Hurricane is refuelled on the flight line at Tangmere. Note the massive wooden two-bladed Watts fixed pitch propeller, later replaced by three-bladed variable pitch airscrews.

Far from the home comforts of Tangmere, with its well-equipped and spacious hangars, these 1 Squadron fitters struggle with an open-air engine change in France during the spring of 1940. Harsh conditions, frequent moves of aerodrome and a heavy attrition rate left pilots and groundcrews tired and battle-weary.

Home from home! Although it is hardly as splendid as Tangmere's mess, these 1 Squadron pilots have requisitioned a French bungalow to use as a temporary mess and they are pictured relaxing in the spring sunshine as the German war machine rolls inexorably toward them. Soon, they would be back at Tangmere again.

LAC Puttick warms up the engine of a 238 Squadron Hurricane at Tangmere in June 1940, at about the time of th
Dunkirk evacuation. 238 Squadron was only at Tangmere for a short while, spending the Battle of Britain period a
Middle Wallop. Note the tented accommodation in the background and the adjacent starter trolley.

CHAPTER FOUR

BATTLE OF BRITAIN: 1940

Tangmere's 'finest hour' was undoubtedly in the Battle of Britain, from 10 July to 31 October 1940, and 43 Squadron was at the forefront of the action from its Tangmere base. Here, Sgt Buck, Flg Off. Woods-Scawen, Flt Lt Hull, P/O Wilkinson and Sgt Garton pose with a squadron Hurricane. Buck, Woods-Scawen and Hull were all killed in the battle which exacted a heavy toll on all the Tangmere squadrons as they struggled to hold off the mighty Luftwaffe in daily air battles across the south of England. Tangmere, a key sector station, played a crucial and strategic role in 'holding the line' but was itself subjected to devastating air attacks, suffering heavy damage and loss of life. The number of enemy aircraft destroyed was high and many came crashing to earth in the vicinity of Tangmere itself.

The wreckage of a burnt-out Heinkel III on East Beach, Selsey, 11 July 1940. It was shot down by Hurricanes of 145 Squadron from Tangmere's satellite field at Westhampnett. Two of the five crew were killed and were buried in Tangmere churchyard. They were the first of many.

Armourers reload the .303 Browning machine-guns of a 601 Squadron Hurricane at Tangmere during August 1940 as an engine fitter replaces the top engine cowl. A quick turn-around between sorties was essential if squadrons were to remain effective and operational.

Stuka! Aircrews supervise the loading of a 250 kg bomb beneath a Junkers Ju 87 Stuka of St.G.77. Aircraft of this type mounted a vicious air raid on RAF Tangmere on 16 August 1940, causing heavy damage and loss of life, but Tangmere's defenders dealt with them harshly.

A huge pillar of fire and smoke rises above a battered Tangmere on 16 August 1940. This picture was taken from Colworth on the Bognor Road. Despite the mayhem caused by the Stuka attacks, the aerodrome remained operational. The medical officer and two airmen/medical orderlies received the Military Cross and Military Medal respectively for heroism in the face of the enemy.

Raiding the raiders! At Bowley Farm, South Mundham, South African Flt Lt Carl Davies of 601 Squadron sent one of the Tangmere attackers crashing down through the trees. Here soldiers strip ammunition out of the wrecked Stuka.

This Heinkel III was shot down by Sgt Pilot Whall in a Spitfire from Westhampnett, and it crashed on the beach at West Wittering on 26 August 1940. Before it could be salvaged time and tide sucked it beneath the sand, although some parts were recovered in the 1970s.

This gaping crater in the pavement of Woodhouse Road, Hove, marked the impact point of a 43 Squadron Hurricane which was shot down on 30 August 1940, burying itself deep in the ground.

The Hurricane's unfortunate pilot was twenty-year-old Sgt Dennis Noble. He was officially buried in 1940 at his home town of Retford, but his remains were discovered in the wreckage of his Hurricane in 1996. Aware that he was still with his aeroplane, a number of wartime research groups and museums had declined to recover the buried wreckage.

Pilots of 43 Squadron awaiting the order to 'scramble' outside their dispersal point hut in 1940. Sgt Dennis Noble stands in the doorway. Seated is the CO, Sqn Ldr 'Tubby' Badger; shot down and badly injured on 30 August 1940, he succumbed to his wounds on 30 June 1941.

Soldiers examine the propeller from a crashed Junkers 88, shot down at Bosham by Tangmere-based fighters on 21 September 1940. The four crew were all captured unhurt. Half a century later the pilot, Kurt Sodemann, revisited the scene.

P/O Franek Surma (left) and Flg Off. 'Chatty' Bowen larking around, making mock Nazi salutes, at their 607 Squadron dispersal hut. Bowen's aircraft vanished near the Isle of Wight on 1 October 1940, and Surma's over the Channel on 8 November 1941. No trace of either was ever found. Note the 'captured' Mae-West worn by Bowen; German life-jackets were considered superior to British ones.

Safely back at his Tangmere base, Sgt Deller of 43 Squadron laughs off his escape from his crippled Hurricane on 7 September 1940. It was, though, a black day for the squadron, with two other pilots being killed.

A scene typical of the period as weaving fighters at high altitude tangle a pattern of vapour trails above Bognor Regis in 1940. The defending fighters were certainly Tangmere-based and times like these were very often the only chance groundcrews had to see 'their' pilots and aeroplanes in action.

Hurricane P2728 of 607 Squadron was shot down when flying from Tangmere on 9 September 1940. Lost for over thirty years, it was finally discovered buried in a ditch at Bockingfold Farm, Goudhurst, in 1971. Its twenty-year-old South African pilot, P/O George James Drake, was still in the cockpit. He was buried with full military honours at Brookwood Military Cemetery, Surrey, in 1972. (This photograph of P2728 was not taken at Tangmere.)

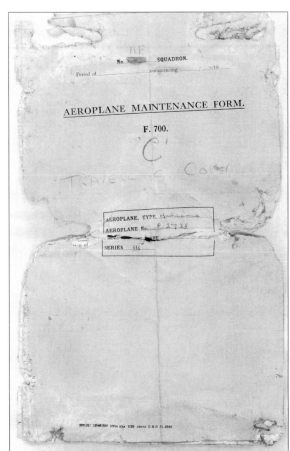

Missed by the recovery team in 1971, this RAF Form 700, still legible, was discovered at the bottom of the same ditch in November 1997. Remarkably, it was still intact and all the entries made nearly sixty years previously at Tangmere could still be read!

South African Carl Davies (see page 42) was shot down and killed while flying from Tangmere on 6 September 1940. His 601 Squadron Hurricane crashed into the back garden of Canterbury Cottage, Brenchley, Kent. This photograph shows the burnt-out remains of his Hurricane in the garden, with Davis's unused parachute covering over the unfortunate airman's body.

MOTOR C

ROAD TRAFFIC ACT 1930 TO 1934.

Certificate of Insurance.

Certificate No. H.F.D. Y 4839/52566

1. Index Mark and Registration Number of Vehicle Insured ... ...   CKL. 148

2. Name of Policyholder   ...   C.R.Davis Esq.

3. Effective Date of the Commencement of Insurance for the purposes of the Act   28th September, 1939

    Date of Expiry of Insurance   ...   14th September, 1940

5. Persons or Classes of Persons Entitled to Drive ... ...   The Policyholder. The Policyholder may also drive a ...cle not belonging to him

...he person driving holds a ... ...the Vehicle or is ...holding or obtaining s...

...tions as to use ... ...e private or business or ...e purpo...e Policyholder, also use for ...ion ...

Policy does not cover use for Hiring, Racing, Pace-making, or Speed Testing.

...imitations rendered inoperative by Section 12 of the Road Traffic Act 1934 are not to be this heading.

I Hereby Certify that the Policy to which this is issued in accordance with the provisions of Part II. Acts 1930 to 1934.

For and on behalf of LLOYD'S UNDERWRIT...,

THE "H.P." MOTOR POLICIES

LLOYD'S

...church Street, ...on, E.C.3.

TELEPHONE: MANSION HOUSE 3017.
TELEGRAMS: POLANPOL, FE...ONDON.

This poignant document, charred around the edges, was Carl Davis's Motor Insurance Certificate, retrieved from the burnt-out cockpit of his aeroplane at Canterbury Cottage. It expired shortly afterwards, on 14 September.

P/O Percy Burton, a 23-year-old South African, lies buried at St Andrew's Church, Tangmere, although he was not a Tangmere-based pilot. Flying a Hurricane from North Weald with 249 Squadron, he rammed a Messerschmitt 110 over Hailsham, Sussex, on 27 September 1940 and was killed in the subsequent crash. He was buried at Tangmere because it was the nearest RAF burial ground to his place of death. Interestingly, Burton was recommended for the Victoria Cross for ramming the German but the award was never made.

Sgt Pilot Mervyn Sprague, aged twenty-one, was shot down over the Channel in his 602 Squadron Spitfire on 11 September 1940; his body was washed ashore at Brighton on 10 October 1940. In the intervening period his distraught widow kept a daily vigil outside his Westhampnett base. He now lies buried at St Andrew's, Tangmere.

Ulsterman Sgt Julius Holland from Bangor was an Observer on board a Blenheim bomber which was shot down into the Channel off the French coast during August 1940. Washed ashore on the Sussex coast, his body was buried at St Andrew's, Tangmere.

Although not taken at Tangmere, this photograph of a tipped-up 43 Squadron Hurricane in May 1940 has a double Tangmere significance. Its pilot at the time of this incident was P/O Oelofse, who was killed flying from Tangmere on 8 August 1940, and lies buried at St Andrew's. On 7 October 1940 this same aeroplane (L1728) was in the hands of 607 Squadron, Tangmere, when it collided with another Hurricane and crashed at Slindon, killing its pilot, Flg Off. I.B. Difford, who also lies buried at St Andrew's.

CHAPTER FIVE

THE WAR YEARS: 1941–45

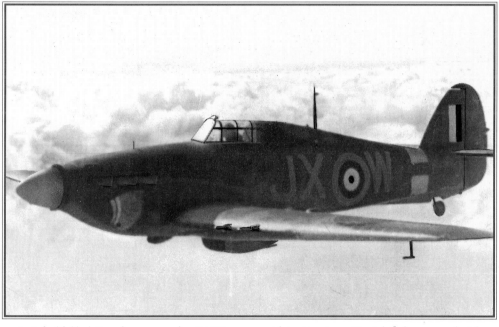

In July 1941, 1 Squadron returned to RAF Tangmere with its Hurricane IIc nightfighters, armed with cannon. JX-W was flown by Canadian Sgt Pilot Scott and carried an impressive Indian Chief's head on the engine cowling. From 1941 onwards there was a shift in emphasis at Tangmere from purely defensive to offensive fighter actions. Fighter-bomber missions to France were regularly flown from the airfield, as were 'intruder' night-operations and fighter cover sorties for day bomber raids. In addition, the airfield saw an increasing number of visiting aircraft: damaged, lost, out of fuel or diverted from home bases. Highly secret missions were also flown in and out of Tangmere by Lysander aircraft delivering and collecting SOE agents from occupied France. The airfield also played a pivotal role in the achievement of air superiority in the Dieppe raid and later on D-Day.

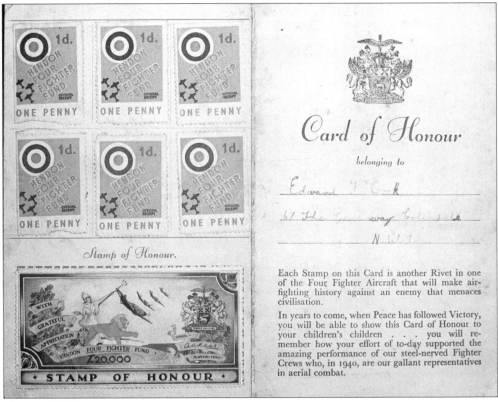

Stamp of Honour.

Card of Honour

belonging to

Edward F Cook

61 The ___way ___

N.W.9

STAMP OF HONOUR

Each Stamp on this Card is another Rivet in one of the Four Fighter Aircraft that will make air-fighting history against an enemy that menaces civilisation.

In years to come, when Peace has followed Victory, you will be able to show this Card of Honour to your children's children . . . you will re-member how your effort of to-day supported the amazing performance of our steel-nerved Fighter Crews who, in 1940, are our gallant representatives in aerial combat.

Towns and communities often clubbed together to purchase presentation aircraft from so-called Spitfire Funds. Hendon ran a Four Fighter Fund, and one of the Spitfires purchased was W3333 *Hendon Pegasus*, a MkV aeroplane, which was delivered to 129 Squadron at Tangmere's satellite airfield at Westhampnett. This was the fund savings card for the patriotic citizens of Hendon.

Unfortunately, the life of *Hendon Pegasus* was short. On 7 September 1941 it collided with another squadron Spitfire after take-off. The other Spitfire, flown by P/O Cunliffe, managed a forced landing back at Westhampnett, but W3333 plunged into Chichester Harbour at Birdham Lock after Sgt Pilot Boddy had taken to his parachute. In recent years the author has been involved in recovering the remains of Spitfire W3333.

Equipped with Spitfires, 65 Squadron was based at Tangmere from November 1940 to February 1941. Here, Sgt Pilot McPherson poses with his machine, YT-J, and his groundcrew, fitter LAC Jones and rigger LAC Webb. Fitters and riggers were generally assigned to a particular aeroplane and pilot and they formed a close-knit team, the groundcrews taking a keen interest and pride in 'their' aeroplane and pilot.

616 Squadron formed part of the Tangmere (Spitfire) Wing during the spring and summer of 1941. This aeroplane flew from Tangmere down to Friston for forward operation, but while landing into the early morning sun it hit a ridge and crashed. The pilot was unhurt. White sheets were laid out on the wings and fuselage to serve as visibility markers for other aircraft using the strip.

The pilots of 616 Squadron at Tangmere pictured in early 1941 outside their dispersal hut. Typical are the pipes, scarves, leather jackets and the inevitable mascot dog! This would have been the entire complement of squadron pilots, and although the Battle of Britain was over the attrition rate was still high.

Sgt Pilot Ben Bingley of 616 Squadron died when his Spitfire dived vertically out of formation from over 20,000 ft, plunging into the ground north of Worthing on 10 March 1941. Oxygen failure was the most likely cause. Bingley, a 24-year-old hospital administrator from Leicester, lies buried at St Andrew's, Tangmere.

On 21 April 1942, 234 Squadron flew down from Ibsley to operate from Tangmere for a sortie over Northern France. Three Danish presentation Spitfires were with the Squadron: *Skagen Ind* (shown here), *Niels Ebbesen* and *Valdemar Atterdag*. Unfortunately, *Valdemar Atterdag*, flown by Danish P/O Axel Svendsen, failed to return. In 1995 Svendsen's family presented a replica of his Spitfire to Tangmere Museum.

This is Spitfire P7836, QJ-K, of 616 Squadron, pictured with its pilot in one of the dispersal 'E' pens on Tangmere's eastern boundary. This aeroplane survived a long history of action with two operational squadrons and three training units before being struck-off in January 1945.

King George VI and Queen Elizabeth visited RAF Tangmere for a field investiture on 14 July 1944. They are included in this group photograph outside the officers' mess. The senior officers in the group were not all from Tangmere but would have travelled to the station from other units or bases for the occasion.

This was the 'Q' airfield, a dummy or decoy aerodrome situated at West Wittering in Sussex, to entice enemy raiders away from Tangmere. At night it would show airfield lights, illuminations from dummy aeroplanes and cars, and other signs of activity. Whether it ever fooled the enemy is uncertain!

Spitfires of 65 Squadron dispersed and tied down against the wind at Westhampnett. Now Goodwood Airport, this aerodrome was an important part of Tangmere's administrative infrastructure and had few of the permanent facilities established at Tangmere. It was abandoned by the RAF at the war's end.

A 'night school' under way in 1 Squadron's crewroom at Tangmere in 1942: (from left to right) Sgt Prideaux-Bruse, Sgt Travis, Sgt Smith, Flt Lt Crabb, P/O Corbett, Sqn Ldr MacLachlan. 'One Armed Mac', as he was known, had lost his left arm in action but had a special device fitted to allow him to operate the Hurricane's throttles. He was eventually killed in action over France.

Tangmere from approximately 10,000ft on 17 June 1941. Bomb damage from the Stuka raid of the previous August can still be clearly seen, as can a number of 'dispersed' Westland Whirwind fighters of 263 Squadron. Only one-and-a-bit of the original Belfast hangars remain standing, and the runways and the field itself have been painted with decoy hedges and fields.

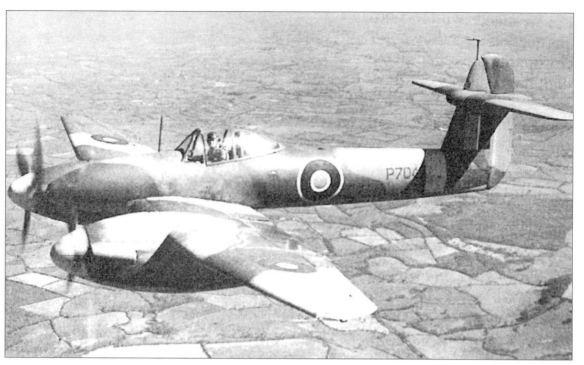

Westland Whirlwind P7047 of 263 Squadron crashed on approach to Tangmere on 8 October 1943, killing its pilot when it came down near the village of Oving.

The RAF and WAAF contingent from Tangmere take part in a War Weapons Week parade at Chichester Cathedral during 1941.

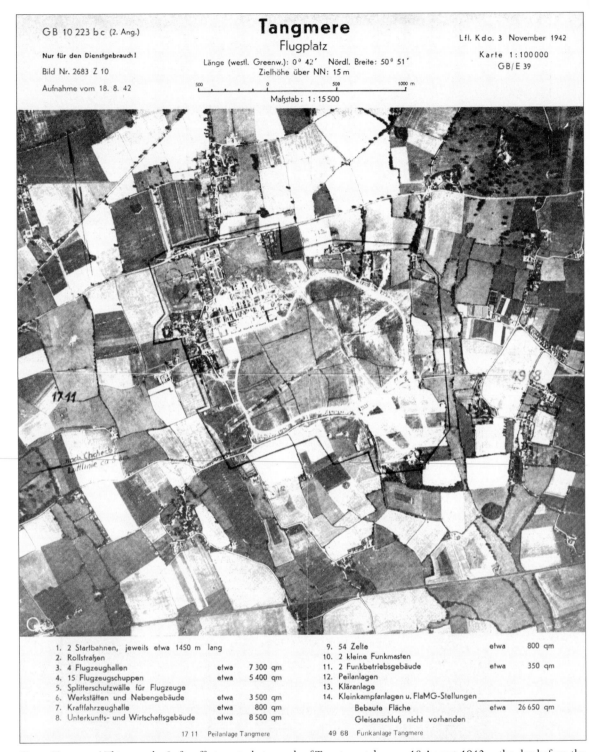

Tangmere
Flugplatz

Länge (westl. Greenw.): 0° 42′   Nördl. Breite: 50° 51′
Zielhöhe über NN: 15 m

500   0   500   1000 m

Maßstab: 1 : 15500

1. 2 Startbahnen, jeweils etwa 1450 m lang			9. 54 Zelte	etwa	800 qm
2. Rollstraßen			10. 2 kleine Funkmasten		
3. 4 Flugzeughallen	etwa	7 300 qm	11. 2 Funkbetriebsgebäude	etwa	350 qm
4. 15 Flugzeugschuppen	etwa	5 400 qm	12. Peilanlagen		
5. Splitterschutzwälle für Flugzeuge			13. Kläranlage		
6. Werkstätten und Nebengebäude	etwa	3 500 qm	14. Kleinkampfanlagen u. FlaMG-Stellungen		
7. Kraftfahrzeughalle	etwa	800 qm	Bebaute Fläche	etwa	26 650 qm
8. Unterkunfts- und Wirtschaftsgebäude	etwa	8 500 qm	Gleisanschluß nicht vorhanden		

17 11   Peilanlage Tangmere   49 68   Funkanlage Tangmere

Target Tangmere! This was the Luftwaffe target photograph of Tangmere taken on 18 August 1942 – the day before the Dieppe Raid. Runway extensions are under way and the picture makes an interesting comparison with that on page 58. Annotations identify individual buildings and features – clearly the camouflage had not fooled the Germans!

TANGMERE AERODROME.

DETAILED COST OF 6" UNREINFORCED CONCRETE RUNWAY.

Measurements taken on Thursday December 17th 1942.

Battery of Mixers comprising 1 14/10 and 2 10/7

Working day of 8 hours. Machine time 6½ hours. Output 116.6 cu.yds.

Area 420'x 15' = 700 sq.yds

Batches for 14/10 Machine 168	Batches for 2 10/7 Machines 334	
Mix. 1.2½.5 i.e. 1.4½.9	Mix. 1.2½.5 i.e. 1½.3.6.	
Quantities for 168 batches	Quantities for 334 batches	
12ton. 12cwt. cement @ 59/7 37. 11. 0.	16ton. 14cwt. cement @ 59/7 49. 15.0.	
28cu.yds. sand @ 11/3 15. 15. 0.	37cu.yds. sand @ 11/3 20. 16.3.	
56cu.yds. ballast @ 7/4 20. 10. 8.	74cu.yds. ballast @ 7/4 27. 2.8	
73. 16. 8.	97. 13.11	
15galls Petrol for 3 mixers 1. 8. 9.	75. 5.5	
£75. 5. 5.	£172. 19.4	

LABOUR

				£.	s.	d.
1 Ganger 8 hours	= 8 hrs. @ 1/10½d	=		15.	0.	
3 Mixer Drivers 8 hrs	=24 hrs. @ 1/6½d	=	1.	17.	0.	
2 Sub Gangers 8 hrs	=16 hrs. @ 1/10½d	=	1.	10.	0.	
3 Labourers 8 hrs	=24 hrs. @ 1/6½d	=	1.	17.	0.	
1 -do- 8 hrs	= 8 hrs. @ 1/6d	=		12.	0.	
1 -do- 8 hrs	= 8 hrs. @ 1/7d	=		12.	8.	
16 -do- 8 hrs	=128hrs. @ 1/5½d	=	9.	6.	8.	
			16.	10.	4.	
33 bonus @ 1/2d per day			1.	18.	6.	
27 C.C.Insurance Contributions @ 3½d				7.	11.	
			18.	16.	9.	
3.2% Workmens Compensations etc.				12.	10.	
			£20.	9.	7.	

HAULAGE AND PLANT

		£.	s.	d.
Haulage 6 dumpers 1 day (8hrs) @ 10/-p.h. @£4 =		24.	0.	0.
1 bulldozer 4 hrs. @ £1 -do- =		4.	0.	0.
Concrete Mixer 14/10 @ 2/6d per.hr. 8 hrs. =		1.	0.	0.
2 x 10/7 @ 2/- per.hr. 8 hrs. =		1.	12.	0.
		30.	12.	0.
Miscellaneous Haulage		3.	0.	0.
		£33.	12.	0.

CURING

		£.	s.	d.
4 men 6hrs. @ 1/6d inclusive	=	1.	16.	0.
Colas 100 galls. @ 10.875	=	4.	10.	6.
Hire Sprayer 1 day	=		10.	0.
Consumable Hessian 1/10 (700 sq.yds. @ 1/-)	=	3.	10.	0.
		£10.	6.	6.

SUMMARY OF COSTS.

	£.	s.	d.
Labour	20.	9.	7.
Materials	172.	19.	4.
Haulage and Plant	33.	12.	0.
Curing	10.	6.	6.
Form Setting	4.	1.	8.
	241	9.	1.
1½% Small Plant & Tools	3.	10.	11.
	£245.	0.	0.

The cost of runway extension works at Tangmere, dated December 1942. By today's standards, the sum of £245 seems a very reasonable one!

AID TO RUSSIA FUND

A

Grand Dance

will be held at the

UNICORN HOTEL

on

Wednesday, Dec. 10th

Dancing 7.30 to 11.45

R.A.F. (Tangmere) Dance Band

(Members of the late Ken Johnson's Dance Band
from Cafe de Paris, W. 1)

(Under the direction of John Allen)

By kind permission of the Commanding Officer

Admission 5/6 (including Refreshments)

Licence applied for

Tickets obtainable from The Unicorn

Moore & Wingham, Printers, 39 East Street.   Tel. 2883

A Grand Dance for the 'Aid To Russia Fund' was sure to be a popular event for Tangmere personnel, held as it was in the Unicorn Hotel, Chichester, a regular haunt of airmen from the base. Landlord Arthur King reserved a special welcome for his 'Tangmere boys'.

Some of the pilots of 1 Squadron 'at readiness' in their Tangmere crewroom. Typical are the armchairs and the pot-bellied stove which were a welcome source of comfort in an otherwise austere environment. Long hours could be spent here, awaiting the call to action.

The Belgian Sqn Ldr Le-Roy DuVivier flew with 43 Squadron during the Battle of Britain and on 19 August 1942 he led the squadron from Tangmere into action over Dieppe, covering the beachhead landings.

Pilots of 41, 43, 66 and 118 and 501 Squadrons celebrate their successful return to Tangmere after the Dieppe operation on 19 August 1942. More than 400 hours of flying were logged by the five squadrons during this epic day.

Pilots from six nations flew with 43 Squadron from Tangmere on the Dieppe operation of 19 August 1942. Pictured from left to right are a Pole, an Australian, a Gold Coast National, a Canadian, an American and a New Zealander. Although this is a posed photograph, no other picture could illustrate so well the truly multi-national nature of the war effort.

Pilots and groundcrew of 181 Squadron, 1943. Popularly known as a 'Bombphoon' to the press, the Typhoon soon proved itself to be a devastating ground-attack fighter; it was in its element after the D-Day landings as it excelled at 'tank-busting' and destroying fortified emplacements, vehicle convoys and so on.

The tragedy of war. On 22 April 1943 Sgt Pilot E.H. Fletcher of 197 Squadron, Tangmere, lost his life when his Typhoon spun out of control, crashing into Beatty Road, Bognor Regis, killing Leonard Martlew in his garden and injuring Miss Daisy Smith. Here, firemen and other rescuers pick through the smouldering wreckage of the fighter.

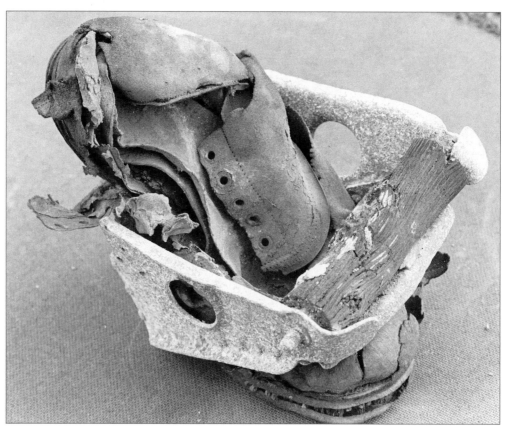

Another tragedy. This grim relic was found on the beach near Littlehampton and is the rudder pedal of a Typhoon – probably a Tangmere-based machine. Trapped in the pedal is the pilot's boot, telling its own awful story.

An aeronautical rarity, this Martin Maryland bomber crashed on take-off from Tangmere while en route for a delivery flight to Malta. The crew survived.

The hutted dispersal point of 486 (Typhoon) Squadron on the eastern boundary of Tangmere in 1943. These wooden Air Ministry huts remained in use long after the war ended. The immaculately kept lawns and flower beds were tended by aircrews and groundcrews in off-duty hours!

Perhaps the most secret address in wartime Sussex was Tangmere Cottage. Opposite the station gate, this was the closely guarded base of 161 (Special Duties) Squadron which flew agents in and out of France under cover of darkness. These secret and hazardous missions were flown by Lysander aircraft, detached from their Tempsford base and hidden away in the remote south-west corner of Tangmere aerodrome. Here, the squadron pilots and groundcrew pose for a rare group shot.

Not all missions to collect agents, known as 'Joes', from France went according to plan. Lysander T1508 had tipped up and clearly would not be coming home. Under the noses of the Germans the aeroplane was destroyed, but not before a brave photographer had snapped the scene.

This 'Most Secret' snapshot of T1508 shows the aircraft's black finish, rear passenger compartment and the ladder to the rear cockpit. There was also an extra fuel tank beneath the fuselage. Note the peculiar 'shepherd's crook' device below the fuselage which was used to pick up, or snatch, message packages from the ground.

There was also a human cost to these missions. Although the occupants of T1508 survived and returned home, two returning Lysanders crashed near Tangmere in fog on 16/17 December 1943, killing both pilots and several French agents. Albert Berthaud was one of the casualties that night.

Jacques Tayar was another of the casualties on that tragic night. Both men are buried in the French plot of Brookwood Military Cemetery, Surrey. The part played by such agents in bringing about the success of D-Day in 1944 cannot be underestimated.

The Australian Flg Off. Ted Hall of 129 (Mysore) Squadron, based at Westhampnett, was forced to bale out of his flak-damaged Spitfire above Arlington, Sussex, on 5 May 1942. Such was his affection for his wartime station that Ted named his Queensland house Tangmere when he returned home.

In 1976 the wreckage of Ted's Spitfire was found buried in the Wealden clay at Endlewick Farm. Amazingly, his flying helmet and goggles, well preserved, were found in the wreckage of the cockpit.

In October 1943, 41 Squadron brought its new clipped wing Spitfires to Tangmere and posed for this group photograph. Four of the pilots are probably at 'readiness', or have just returned from a sortie as they wear Mae Wests and flying kit. The photograph includes French and Australian pilots, and the squadron chaplain is at the extreme right.

The Duchess of Gloucester visited Tangmere in 1944 to open a new underground telephone exchange building.

Pilots of 91 Squadron at Tangmere in October 1943 or February 1944. The Tangmere control tower can clearly be seen under construction in the background. Many people assert that this building is postwar — this picture disproves that theory!

A corporal airman ignites a signal rocket at night on the RAF Tangmere control tower balcony.

The control tower crew at Tangmere in 1945. The complement includes WAAFs and at least some qualified flying personnel. Their role was purely air traffic control and airfield movements; they were not operational or tactical fighter controllers.

As Tangmere's fighter squadrons went hunting over France on 19 August 1942, a Junkers 88 came snooping over Tangmere but flew headlong into the Sussex Downs above West Dean, smashing itself and its four occupants to pieces. This was all that remained.

TANGMERE THEATRE

(By kind permission of Officer Commanding)

presents

DIANA WYNYARD   ANTON WALBROOK

ATHENE SEYLER   MARGARETTA SCOTT

in

WATCH on the RHINE

by

LILLIAN HELLMAN

Author of " The Little Foxes " and " The Children Hour '

Sunday, September 19th, 1943

at 18.30 hrs.

Willis', Printers, Chichester

Entertainment was an important feature in the lives of all wartime servicemen and women. Tangmere Theatre presented a Lillian Hellman play, *Watch on the Rhine*, in September 1943.

R.A.F.
STATION TANGMERE

Christmas 1943

*The Commanding Officer & Officers
wish you all A Happy Christmas*

MENU

Soup

Roast Stuffed Turkey
Roast Pork
Sausages
Apple Sauce
Crisp Potatoes   Brussel Sprouts

Christmas Pudding

Apples

Minerals   Ales   Cigarettes

This was the Christmas menu for other ranks in 1943. Despite shortages and rationing, seasonal fare was still on the menu. Traditionally, the men were served by their officers at Christmas.

A visiting Short Stirling bomber, damaged or out of fuel after a raid over Germany, is captured by an artist at Tangmere in 1943. In the distance is one of several temporary Blister hangars used at Tangmere during this period.

Gp Capt. C.H. Appleton DSO, DFC was Station Commander at Tangmere between January and September 1942. This portrait was drawn by the renowned artist and sculptor Eric Kennington.

Another Kennington portrait, this is Wg Cdr P.R. 'Johnnie' Walker DSO, DFC, a peacetime pilot with 1 Squadron at Tangmere. This portrait was done in 1942 when Walker was Tangmere's Wing Commander Flying. From February to September 1944 he was Station Commander.

NAAFI girls Tania and Elsie in the cockpit of a 303 (Polish) Squadron Spitfire at Westhampnett. The T2 hangar still stand today in the corner of what is now Goodwood Airport, Chichester.

On 5 June 1944, the eve of D-Day, a padre conducted an open-air service for airmen at RAF Tangmere. The next twenty-four hours were, arguably, the most momentous in modern history. The sense of history was certainly not lost on those involved in this great campaign.

Visiting Miles Master aircraft lined up at Tangmere during the summer of 1945.

An unidentified wing commander seated in the cockpit of his Spitfire at Tangmere, 1945. At this time the privilege of rank allowed wing commanders to carry their initials on their aeroplanes. Therefore RT can be assumed to be this pilot's initials.

This Spitfire LF XVI was photographed at Tangmere during the summer of 1945. The Blister hangar behind it stood roughly on the site now occupied by Tangmere Museum.

This Liberator FS-R of 148 Squadron was photographed at Tangmere in the summer of 1945, en route to Foggia, its Italian base. It may have been involved in troop transport duties.

A Beaufighter IV F of the Fighter Interception Unit, Tangmere, photographed in one of the northern perimeter blast pens.

Wellington GR XIII NB855 of the Fighter Interception Unit seems to have suffered a minor mishap at Tangmere during the summer of 1945.

A captured Junkers 88G-6 at the Central Fighter Establishment at Tangmere, 1945. This shot also corresponds roughly with the position of Tangmere Museum.

Another captured enemy machine at Tangmere, this is a Heinkel 219. Sadly, this rare aeroplane was scrapped in around 1947.

Flg Off. William A. Johnson was medical officer at Tangmere for much of the Second World War. As MO for a large permanent station, with many resident squadrons, he was assured of a busy time. Note the Medical Branch flashes above his Volunteer Reserve tabs.

Unfortunately the chalked graffiti on the propellers of this captured Junkers 88 at Tangmere defy all attempts to decipher them! Like most captured enemy aircraft, this aeroplane would have been scrapped.

CHAPTER SIX

POSTWAR TO CLOSURE: 1946–70

This aerial shot of RAF Tangmere was taken in 1949 and makes an interesting comparison with those on pages 58 and 60. Runway extensions, started in 1942, have grown yet further to facilitate jet operations and now extend to the south-west and south-east. Little evidence remains of the wartime damage or camouflage, although the hangars have yet to be rebuilt. The south-west extension not only resulted in the demolition of the Tangmere Hotel, but also cut off the direct road through to Oving village, resulting in an enforced detour via Shopwyke. Although it was still a fighter airfield, the reality was that Tangmere's relevance, or strategic importance, was now gone: the threat was now from the east across the North Sea. For some twenty years the fame of this airfield surpassed that of most others, and it was no less famous than Biggin Hill or Scampton. Now, in the 1990s, the flying field has gone and modern development has swept aside most of what can be seen in this photograph, although the part it played in history and in the development of aviation will never be forgotten.

The Gloster Meteor was the first jet fighter in service with the Royal Air Force and 222 Squadron operated the type from Tangmere between June 1947 and July 1948. At this time the wartime camouflage paint scheme was still in use, but very soon the colourful pre-war silver was adopted once more, reflecting something of the glorious biplane era of some ten years previously. It is hard to believe that in less than a decade fighter aircraft had gone from wood and fabric-built open cockpit biplanes to high-tech, high-performance jets! This particular high-performance jet, Meteor EE467 ZD-Q, lost an argument with the perimeter fence and a ditch at Tangmere and was probably written off, although the pilot was unharmed in what is believed to be the first jet accident on the station.

The pilot poses rather proudly with his bent Meteor as it is ignominiously carted away on a Queen Mary low-loader trailer.

A party of Royal Navy officers visited Tangmere in 1949. The line-up includes HRH the Duke of Edinburgh, marked with the small 'x'. The large number 25 boards on the control tower indicate which runway is in use.

A Mosquito NF 36 of 85 Squadron, based at West Malling, visited Tangmere in about 1949. At this time 85 Squadron was a nightfighter unit and the Mosquito's life was coming to an end as the next generation of nightfighters, Meteor jets, was coming into use.

Another Tangmere visitor at around this time was the sleek De Havilland Hornet, the successor to the Mosquito. Arguably the best-looking twin-engined fighter ever built, the type had only a short service history and no Hornet squadron was based at Tangmere. Sadly, not one single Hornet survives today.

Spitfire SL721, the personal aircraft of ACM Sir James Milne Robb GCB, KDBE, DSO, DFC, visited Tangmere several times in the late 1940s. Its pilot's rank earned him the privilege of having his initials as the aircraft's code letters.

By the early 1960s JMR was in private hands just down the road from Tangmere at Swandean Garage, Worthing; its new owner ran up the engine on Battle of Britain Day every year. For a while SL721 was at the National Motor Museum before going to the USA.

Yet another Tangmere visitor, this is a Royal Navy Fairey Firefly. The tail codes show it was a Ford-based aircraft. Aircraft from this neighbouring Royal Naval Air Station were frequent visitors to Tangmere. The date is probably around 1953.

Another visitor, a 217 Squadron Lockheed Neptune, also in around 1953. Still in the Coastal Command role, 217 Squadron had been based at Tangmere with Avro Ansons fourteen years earlier.

Tribute was paid to RAF Tangmere by the British Railways Board in 1947 with the naming of a 'Battle of Britain' class locomotive, no. 34067, *Tangmere*. This detail shows the station crest on the cab side. Fortunately, this engine survives with the Mid-Hants Railway.

In 1954 this collection of vehicles and trailers housed the Ground-Controlled Approach System alongside Runway 25/07.

These Republic P-47 Thunderbolt fighters of the United States Air Force dropped into Tangmere while participating in air defence exercises in 1949. These long-range fighters excelled during the Second World War and earned themselves the nickname 'Jug'. These were from the 86th Fighter Group based at Neubiberg in Germany.

Bad Penny, a USAF B-29 Superfortress, also turned up at Tangmere during the same air exercises and was probably the largest aeroplane to have used the airfield up to this time.

On 23 December 1949 a Wellington T10 trainer caught fire over the English Channel and made a forced landing at Tangmere. With the fabric burnt away the Wellington's unique geodesic structure is exposed. Fortunately, the crew all survived to go home for Christmas leave.

Tangmere's Coles cranes were essential equipment for clearing and lifting wrecks like the burnt-out Wellington. These are pictured in the motor transport section during 1950.

The RAF Fire Service played a very important part in protecting lives and equipment at Tangmere. Here, a foam-producing tender carries out a practice in front of the fire station. Smothering burning aviation fuel very quickly was essential after crashes.

Some of Tangmere's fire crews. The disc hanging from the belt of the second man from the right held an ejector seat safety pin to secure live ejector seats in jet crashes. Knives and axes were also essential equipment for rescue purposes.

601 Squadron returned to Tangmere for summer camp in the late 1940s. This immaculate line-up of Spitfire LF16s is ready for the AOC's inspection. This was probably the last time operational Spitfires were to be seen at Tangmere.

The station communications Anson came to a rather sad end in 1950 when its brakes failed and it over-ran the runway, demolishing the perimeter fence and felling a tree – apparently now growing from the port engine!

Battle of Britain air displays at Tangmere were always popular with members of the public. Not only could the public meet the RAF 'at home', but a variety of new or interesting aircraft types were on view in static parks and in the air. Various dramatic displays were also organized, including ground attack demonstrations, air sea rescues and squadron scrambles. The static park at Tangmere in 1953 was dominated by the massive bulk of an Avro Lincoln bomber, a postwar development of the famous Lancaster. Further along stand a Vickers Varsity and a Handley Page Hastings. None of these machines was Tangmere-based.

This captured Messerschmitt 108 was seen at Tangmere some time during the immediate postwar period and was flown by Air Cmdr Atcherley, the Station Commander.

Vampires of 72 Squadron visit Tangmere from their Hampshire base at RAF Odiham, 1950. In 1937, 72 Squadron was formed at Tangmere with Gloster Gladiators and this was perhaps the squadron's first return visit to Tangmere since that time. Some of the Vampires are in silver finish, others are camouflaged.

Back home and back in the old routine, 43 Squadron flying silver aeroplanes again! This photograph shows the squadron Meteor F4s in formation in 1950, carrying the new unit code letters SW. The fuselage letters were a legacy of wartime and the colourful squadron markings had not yet been introduced.

34 Squadron also moved in with its Meteors in 1954 and this was the line-up of pilots at Tangmere in that year. Several of them sport berets, the latest fashion in headgear for the RAF.

1 Squadron also came back 'home' with its silver Meteors in 1949. The pre-war rivalry of the two squadrons was back on with a vengeance and the two units once again vied with each other for the prestige of being top squadron in RAF Fighter Command.

Other jet types to be seen at Tangmere in the early 1960s included a visiting Valiant V-Bomber (background) and an English Electric Canberra, WT488, which was to become a resident aeroplane with 245 Squadron. See page 135.

Air Wireless Mechanic G. Stone removes the radio set from a 43 Squadron Meteor on the flight line for its daily inspection, 6 July 1950. At this time the radio workshops were situated in the huts that were later occupied by the Tangmere Military Aviation Museum.

This Auster AOP 9 of the Army Air Corps was on display at an RAF Battle of Britain 'At Home Day' at Tangmere in 1960. Throughout the 1950s and '60s Tangmere saw most types of RAF and NATO aircraft passing through at one time or another.

The scattered remains of a Meteor F8 at Tangmere, 9 September 1952. Part of the serial number VZ542 can be seen on the wreckage of this fatal crash.

From the early 1960s a detachment from 22 (Search & Rescue) Squadron operated from Tangmere with its Westland Whirlwind helicopters. These yellow machines became a familiar sight along the Sussex coastline.

From January to August 1950 Maj Donovan F. Smith (seated, centre) of the USAF commanded 1 Squadron at Tangmere. During his period of command RAF squadrons were allowed to adopt the colourful markings of the pre-war era but the huge red chevron on this Meteor was deemed rather too flamboyant and was toned down to a smaller red rectangle.

Lined up at Tangmere in the early 1950s for a Battle of Britain display is a huge range of postwar RAF and NATO aircraft. Perhaps this picture will provide something of a challenge for aircraft recognition enthusiasts?

Meteor VZ440 was the first of 43 Squadron's new F8 versions delivered during 1950. It wears the familiar chequerboard design, last seen in the 1930s at Tangmere on Furies. This particular aeroplane turned out to be a 'rogue' machine and was repeatedly put unserviceable before leaving the squadron.

Definitely unserviceable was this Meteor F8 of 1 Squadron, which landed without wheels at Tangmere in 1951. The red outlined bar became the officially adopted squadron marking in this period.

An inglorious chapter in the history of a glorious squadron. Prior to re-equipment with Meteors in 1948 1 Squadron at Tangmere lost its fighter status and was re-equipped with Harvard and Oxford trainers, becoming an Instrument Flying Training Unit. The yellow Harvards pictured at Tangmere still carry the squadron code letters, JX.

The first jet nightfighter unit in the RAF was 29 Squadron, equipped with Meteor NF11s, photographed airborne from Tangmere in 1951. Camouflage was now reappearing on RAF fighters, but squadron markings were retained. 29 Squadron's markings were red Xs on a white ground with red border.

The aircrews of 29 Squadron lined up for inspection by AM the Earl of Brandon at Tangmere during 1952. The air marshal is chatting with sergeant pilots and aircrew who, at this time, still made up a significant proportion of flying personnel in the RAF. By the 1960s, however, all pilots and aircrew were officers, although a few duties were still held by NCOs. Inspections such as this were loathed by crews, who spent a lot of time preparing for them.

The complement of 1 Squadron, Tangmere, October 1954. A mixture of silver and camouflaged Meteors were on strength at this time and unusually they are lined up nose-to-nose; traditionally they were photographed tail-to-tail. The Meteors of 29 Squadron in the background, however, are tail-to-tail and seem to have stolen 1 Squadron's traditional pose!

This De Havilland Venom visited Tangmere during 1953 and was a rather colourful machine, painted gloss blue overall with a brightly chequered tail section. The unusual colour scheme suggests that the aeroplane formed part of an aerobatic team. However, the chequered tail and the wing commander's pennant below the cockpit indicate that it was the CO's personal machine!

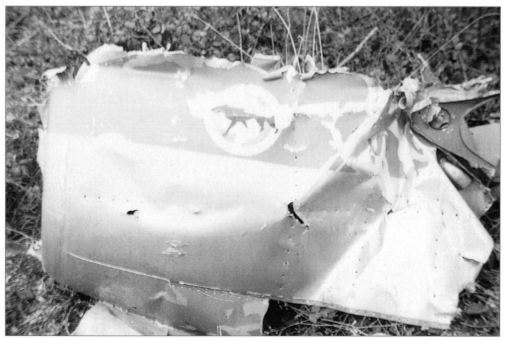

On 3 March 1955 a Sea Vampire from RNAS Ford and a 34 Squadron Meteor from Tangmere collided in mid-air near Arundel. Both pilots were killed. The Meteor crashed into woods at Binstead, and this picture shows the squadron's wolf and moon emblem on part of the wreckage.

Twenty-year-old Sub Lt Carter died in the Sea Vampire, while the Meteor carried 22-year-old Flg Off. Hartnoll to his untimely death. Hartnoll was buried alongside wartime RAF casualties at RAF Tangmere, and the poignant inscription on his headstone reads simply 'He gave happiness'.

An Air Wireless Mechanic puzzles over radio and radar technical publications in what is now the Battle of Britain Hall at Tangmere Military Aviation Museum. In the 1950s and '60s this was the radio repair workshop. One hopes that he isn't about to take out his frustration with his large spanner on the delicate equipment behind him!

This Handley Page Hastings transport aircraft visited Tangmere in 1953. There appears to be some evidence of damage to the leading edge of the tailplane. This was probably the result of some careless ground manoeuvring by this aeroplane or others. Either way, some considerable repair work is clearly in order.

This 1950s parade of squadrons and their equipment at Tangmere is for the benefit of the AOC 11 Group, RAF Fighter Command, who is taking the salute from the saluting base in front of the hangars.

Also on parade are the men and machines of the RAF Tangmere motorcycle club, pictured near the control tower in around 1960. BSAs, Velocettes, Triumphs and Ariels are included in the line-up.

Visiting Bristol Brigand target-towing aircraft were a rare sight at Tangmere in October 1953. They are shown taxiing in on the southern perimeter track.

Hurricanes at Tangmere again, this time in 1951. Five Hurricanes of the Portuguese Air Force were flown in to Tangmere to be used in the making of the Battle of Britain film *Angels One-Five*. Here, the Portuguese pilots are greeted by AM the Earl of Brandon and Gp Capt. Tom Prickett (left), together with the air attaché from the Portuguese Embassy in London.

Under threatening skies this Meteor sits on what became known as the 'Fire Dump' on the far eastern side of RAF Tangmere. It was probably waiting to be torched for fire practice in the 1960s.

25 Squadron, another nightfighter unit, with Meteor NF14s, was based at Tangmere from September 1957 to July 1958 when it was disbanded. This informal group photograph was taken just prior to the squadron's disbandment. 25 Squadron's associations with the station were brief. In this picture, taken on the concrete hangar apron, the NF14's bulbous nose section, containing the radar unit, can be clearly seen. After disbandment, the squadron reformed with Gloster Javelin fighters, a type not associated with Tangmere although the squadron's aircraft did visit the station. Primarily a nightfighter unit throughout its history, the squadron's motto was 'Feriens tego' (Striking, I defend).

All RAF stations had their own communications aircraft, and in the late 1940s and early '50s Tangmere's was this Percival Proctor, seen in its silver livery on a rather wintry day. 'Tangmere' is painted above the cockpit door.

On 24 April 1953 AVM Sir Charles Longcroft presented the first squadron standard in the RAF. Appropriately, this went to 1 Squadron at Tangmere. Here Flg Off. Mike Chandler accepts the standard for the squadron.

Sqn Ldr Neville Duke triumphantly returns to RAF Tangmere on 7 September 1953 in his crimson Hawker Hunter fighter, WB188, after breaking the World Air Speed Record off the Sussex Coast at Littlehampton, achieving a speed of 727.63 mph.

One of the first operational English Electric Canberra bombers in service with the RAF visited Tangmere in the 1950s as part of a tour of stations to show off this new type. Interested personnel curiously inspected the new aeroplane.

In 1955, 34 Squadron changed its Meteors for Hawker Hunters. Here, H-Hotel awaits attention in the servicing hangar at Tangmere, resplendent with its black, gold and white squadron markings beneath the cockpit – perhaps the most eye-catching markings in use at the time and certainly outdoing those of 1 and 43 Squadrons!

As part of the Tangmere wing, 34 Squadron was sent to Cyprus to cover operations during the Suez crisis. In addition to the colourful unit badge, cream and black stripes were applied as identification markings for all Allied aircraft in the Suez operation.

Arriving to take part in the Battle of Britain flying display at Tangmere in 1957 this F-86 Sabre of the Royal Canadian Air Force suffered nose-wheel failure on landing and was towed off the runway on to the grass.

This Beech-18 Expeditor of the Royal Canadian Air Force was an unusual visitor to Tangmere. It brought spares and technicians to deal with the 'bent' F-86 Sabre. The buildings in the background were occupied by Tangmere Aviation Museum in the 1980s.

ROYAL AIR FORCE, TANGMERE

Battle of Britain Flying Programme, 1957

Item No.	Aircraft	Event
1	4 F.100s	Formation aerobatics 'Skyblazers'
2	24 Hunters	Stream take-off
3	Spitfire	Aerobatics
4	4 F.100s	Flypast
5	Hurricane	Aerobatics
6	Gannet	Flypast
7	Provost	Aerobatics
8	3 B.45s	Flypast
9	Helicopter	Rescue Technique
10	4 F.86 Ds	Flypast
11	24 Hunters	Flypast
12	4 Javelins	Flypast
13	24 Hunters	Stream landing
14	Valiant	Flypast
15	Sea Hawk	Aerobatics
16	Vulcan	Flypast
17	Meteor 8	Height and speed competition
18	Hurricane	Aerobatics
19	Britannia	Flypast
20	3 Canberras	Flypast
21	Swift	Demonstration
22	4 Meteors	Flypast
23	Sabres	Formation drill
24	N.113	Flypast
25	Hunter	Aerobatics
26	Helicopter	Comic interlude
27	Glider and Tug	Gliding demonstration
28	R.N. Miscellaneous	Flypast
29	8 Meteor 12/14s	Flypast
30	8 Hunters	Squadron drill
31	Victor	Flypast
32	4 Wyverns	Ground attack, followed by Fire Fighting demonstration

The flying programme for the 1957 Battle of Britain display, RAF Tangmere. New types such as Javelins, F-100s, Vulcans and Valiants were exciting display features, but the mass display by twenty-four Hunters must have been the show's highlight.

ALDERMAN CHARLES TYSON,
B.Sc.,F.C.A.,J.P.
MAYOR

THE MAYOR'S PARLOUR,

TOWN HALL,

BRIGHTON, 1.

14th February, 1958.

Dear David

Years ago Brighton officially adopted No. 1 Fighter Squadron, R.A.F., which is known as "Brighton's Own" Squadron. It is at the moment stationed at Tangmere Aerodrome, near Chichester.

You may have heard of our recently entertaining them, and now the Commanding Officer, Squadron-Leader R. Kingsford, and his Officers have very kindly offered to entertain a party of Brighton children at Tangmere one afternoon - with the idea that you should see something of what the Squadron do and afterwards have tea with them there.

I am writing to invite you to be one of the party to go on this outing. Will you please let me know, at once, on the enclosed slip whether you can, or cannot, accept.

The outing will be on Thursday, 27th February. A Southdown Coach will be at the North end of St. Peter's Church at 12.50 p.m., ready to take the party to Tangmere. Those who accept should meet at the Coach promptly at that time.

It is expected that the Coach will leave Tangmere at 4.45 p.m., and arrive back at St. Peter's Church at about 6 p.m.

The Chairman of the Education Committee has given me his consent to the children concerned being given leave from school; but this letter must be shown to your teacher before you go so that permission can properly be obtained in advance for absence, and, if necessary, to leave early from morning school.

I hope you will be able to take part.

Yours sincerely,

Mayor.

95/113

In the 1930s 1 Squadron at Tangmere had been designated 'Brighton's Own' and in 1958 this was recognized by the Mayor of Brighton who entertained the squadron at the Town Hall. Later, a party of excited Brighton schoolchildren were invited to Tangmere for the day as guests of the squadron.

'qn Ldr R. Kingsford led 1 Squadron, now equipped with Hawker Hunters, in the late 1950s. Here, he poses by his ersonal aircraft, marked with the squadron's 'Flying One' emblem, which is also emblazoned on his 'bone dome' helmet.

This 1 Squadron Hunter has its gun pack re-armed at Tangmere in 1956, shortly before the Suez crisis, during which Tangmere Wing was despatched to Akrotiri in Cyprus to cover operations in Egypt.

In May 1958 1 Squadron returned to Tangmere before moving out for the last time. The Squadron's last month at Tangmere was marred by a tragic accident when two Hunters collided over the sea off Selsey Bill. Flt Lt Paxton and Flg Off. Turner (both in this photograph) were killed. They were the last operational casualties at RAF Tangmere.

In 1960 the Varsities of 115 Squadron replaced the exciting jet fighters in the Tangmere circuit, but the life of the station was already coming to an end. Its final flying use was for signals squadrons.

Some of the Tangmere station 'civvies', 1960. Civilian workers were an important part of the establishment at any RAF airfield and these Air Ministry employees were part of the bricks and works team. Civilians manned telephone exchanges, drove vehicles, maintained buildings and gardens, swept and tidied, and stoked the boilers. When Tangmere closed in 1970 it inevitably had an impact upon the local economy and employment.

This poster advertised the 1963 Battle of Britain Week display at Tangmere. Free admission to air displays is, sadly, a thing of the past!

As with all Battle of Britain displays at Tangmere the 1963 show welcomed a range of visiting aeroplanes, including this Vampire T11 two-seat trainer. Already obsolete by the 1960s, the type remained in service with the RAF well into the 1970s.

The visiting French contingent formed quite an impressive line-up in the static park at the 1963 display. This Mystère of the 12th Escadre, French Air Force, was parked alongside a USAF T-33 Shooting Star, a type currently represented at Tangmere Museum.

The most unusual visitor to the RAF Tangmere display in September 1963 was this Avro 707c delta-wing experimental aircraft, WX744, which doubtless attracted much attention.

A little less aerodynamic was this Morane-Saulnier MS760 Paris jet trainer of the French Air Force, next door in the line-up of the static park aircraft.

Providing transport for the ground-support team of the French Air Force contingent was this Nord Noratlas of the 51st Escadre. This twin-fuselage design was a frequent visitor to the Tangmere of the 1960s.

A visiting De Havilland Chipmunk from an RAF flying training school is dwarfed by a Valiant V-Bomber at the 1963 Tangmere air display. In August 1971, before the final closure of Tangmere's air traffic control, an RAF Chipmunk made the last official flight from Tangmere, flying the short distance to RAF Thorney Island.

In January 1960 the City of Chichester granted Honorary Freedom of the City to RAF Station Tangmere, as commemorated in this parchment scroll. The silver and enamel representation of the City Arms was presented to the officers' mess. When the Station closed in 1970 the scroll was lodged with the City Council, but in 1992 the author secured its return to Tangmere for display in the Museum.

Troops of the Royal Corps of Signals, 38 Group, Tangmere, exercise their rights of the Freedom of the City by marching through the streets of Chichester for a civic occasion during the early 1970s.

This foam-splattered Voodoo fighter of the USAF hit a slight bump in the runway at RAF Tangmere during a landing in April 1962. The high-speed impact sheared both main undercarriage legs: one ended up on the concrete hangar apron, the other by Oving Church!

'Steady . . . steady . . . Drop! . . . Load Gone.' A C-130 Hercules of the Thorney Island-based Operational Conversion Unit makes a practice parachute drop of stores from its open rear cargo door above Tangmere in 1970.

HRH Prince Charles, the Prince of Wales, disembarks from a De Havilland Chipmunk at Tangmere in August 1969, while learning to fly. The crimson Chipmunk, the RAF's primary trainer, was on the strength of the RAF Queen's Flight and survives in 1998 at nearby Shoreham Airport. The building in the background is the RAF Tangmere fire station.

Prince Charles leaves the crew hut adjacent to the control tower at Tangmere. A Beagle Bassett communications aircraft, also of the Queen's Flight, waits on the ramp.

Four pilots of 1 Squadron relax on the grass at Tangmere, 4 April 1968, prior to the last fighter mission flown from the station. On the right is Flt Lt Alan Pollock, who left the formation flight of four Hunters to fly under the top span of Tower Bridge in a headline-grabbing stunt that earned him an early retirement!

Brown jobs at Tangmere! Soldiers of 638 Signals Troop (Air Formation) of the Royal Corps of Signals formed part of 38 Group, RAF, at Tangmere in the 1960s. Here, they come under scrutiny during an inspection by the AOC 38 Group.

Wg Cdr Gray DFC was the last Station Commander at Tangmere. Here, he cuts a cake with an officer's sword to commemorate the fiftieth anniversary of the Royal Air Force in April 1968. Flt Lt Pollock's exploits saw to it that the commemorative occasion went with a little more gusto than a mere cake-cutting ceremony!

CHAPTER SEVEN

CLOSURE, DECLINE AND DECAY: 1971–98

After closure in 1970, 623 Gliding School stayed on at Tangmere until 1975, maintaining an RAF presence at the station. Primarily, the school provided gliding experience (including qualification to glider pilot proficiency) for Air Training Corps cadets. The instructors were generally civilians who held commissions in the RAF Volunteer Reserve. Here, a Slingsby Cadet of 623 Gliding School formates on another above the eastern boundary of Tangmere and the south-east runway extension. This photograph was taken in 1973, long after closure, but the airfield remained in RAF hands and looks neat and well kept. Within a couple of years, dereliction had set in. Today, this part of the airfield is covered with tomato-growing greenhouses.

The Gliding School used this red-and-white chequered caravan for airfield control purposes until the School moved out in 1975. In 1976 the caravan was left mouldering away in a forgotten corner of the airfield, the last tangible link with service flying at Tangmere.

This Piper Pawnee Ag-Wagon crop-spraying aircraft regularly used Tangmere in the 1970s when employed on local farm work for Moonraker Aviation. The massive concrete blast walls of the 1950s fighter dispersal pens provided protection from the weather for the parked aeroplane. In recent years these hugely strong structures have defied efforts to demolish them.

Two years after closure, and the main gate still seemed fairly well kept and the station sign remained *in situ*. For a while, a Royal Naval Signals Unit maintained a presence at Tangmere and the Royal Corps of Military Police conducted training exercises from Chichester Barracks. West Sussex County Council also had offices on the site before all the buildings were finally sold for development.

'Vehicles Must Give Way to Aircraft' commanded this sign inside the main gate. It was still *in situ* in the 1980s, long after all the aeroplanes had gone! The building in the background was known as the old Handley Page hangar and can be seen on page 134. Latterly it was used as the station theatre. Although apparently 'listed', it nevertheless succumbed to the demolition man.

This T2 type hangar was a postwar development on the northern boundary and was used as a maintenance hangar. It is shown here partly dismantled and by the late 1970s it had gone. The picture on page 111 was taken inside this hangar.

Evocative of the wartime period, this Nissen hut (building no. 71) mouldered away beneath the trees close to the control tower in 1979. Its broken windows, the doors creaking in the wind and the ghostly interior created a haunting sense of Tangmere's wartime past.

The view along one of Tangmere's deserted runways towards Goodwood and Trundle Hill in August 1979. To the right of the runway (the eastern perimeter) in the distance are the concrete blast pens; to the left is the control tower. The fading large 'X' painted on the runway indicated 'Runway not in use'.

By the mid-1980s redevelopment had resulted in the demolition of most of Tangmere's buildings. Here, the guardroom has been reduced to rubble, with the wooden roof cupola smashed to the ground and graffiti-daubed with a swastika.

The deserted fire service building at Tangmere in August 1979. Still in good condition this building, like most of the others, finally succumbed to modern development in the early 1980s.

The boiler house with its water towers was a familiar landmark at Tangmere and the tall structure can be spotted in the background of many photographs taken on the airfield. Towering above all of the other buildings, its height necessitated the placement of a red warning beacon on the top. This red light remained illuminated for many years after closure – as did the warning lamp atop an electricity pylon to the north of the A27 by the Winterton Arms.

Typifying the decay and vandalism of the late 1980s, this was the sorry state of the control tower. Compare this view with that on page 85. Once, in the early 1980s, this building was offered to the author by the owners, the Church Commissioners, for a nominal £1.

Before vandals, neglect and the weather had taken their toll, this was the view inside the abandoned roof-top 'glasshouse'. The RAF had stripped out the instrumentation and equipment, but when the site was visited by the author in 1979 there were still maps and charts scattered about, one dated 1944!

Still standing in 1982, this was the old Handley Page hangar, more recently the station theatre. This was, in fact, only a small part of the building which once extended several more bays to the right until it was 'modified' by the German air force on 16 August 1940!

This aerial view of Tangmere shows the station in 1980, before development. The camp area within the solid line has all been demolished for development as a housing estate and business park. The dotted line represents a new road link to the village from the A27, which is now *in situ*. Compare this view with the almost identical one on page 9.

This plot, together with the building, was purchased by Tangmere parish council for allotment development – a plan thwarted by a huge raft of wartime concrete which sat about four inches beneath the surface! Fortunately, the failure of the allotment plan was good news for the embryonic Tangmere Museum, which took over the derelict site in 1980.

During the hunt for museum aircraft this English Electric Canberra on the fire dump at Dunsfold, Surrey, was surveyed by the Tangmere team. They were surprised to discover that WT488 had once been based at Tangmere with 245 Squadron (see page 96). Sadly the aeroplane was beyond economic repair or renovation.

This ex-Danish Air Force Hawker Hunter was, however, salvaged from Dunsfold for Tangmere. Although it was missing various items and pieces of equipment, restoration was soon under way in 1982.

Craned into position, the aeroplane was given a first overhaul and finished in etching primer prior to a new paint scheme.

From wreck to showpiece! The ex-Danish Hunter was painted to represent a machine of 43 Squadron to commemorate that unit's famous and lengthy association with Tangmere, and went on display outside the museum. Resplendent in squadron chequerboards, and with a cartoon 'Fighting Cock' beneath the cockpit, the Hunter is a fitting memento of Tangmere's glorious days as a fighter station (even though 43 Squadron had left Tangmere before re-equipping with the Hunter). At the time of writing (1998), this Hunter is scheduled to leave Tangmere for another home. Fortunately, the museum houses another and rather more prestigious Hunter aircraft.

The culmination of years of achievement at Tangmere Museum came with the acquisition of two extremely historic and significant airframes: Hunter WB188 and Meteor EE549. These aircraft, loaned from the RAF, both broke the World Air Speed Records from Tangmere and had been displayed at the Aerospace Museum, RAF Cosford, Staffordshire. After protracted negotiations the aeroplanes finally arrived at Tangmere Military Aviation Museum in 1992 for display in the museum's newly completed Merston Hall. Here, the fuselage of WB188 arrives on a low-loader with the engine nacelles of EE549 – an exciting moment!

Next, came the fuselage of Meteor EE549 together with WB188's wings. These unusual loads must have turned a few heads as they headed south, and homewards, from Shropshire. The whole operation from negotiation, dismantling and transportation to re-erection and display was a mammoth task lasting several months. These are valuable aeroplanes that had to be handled and displayed in accordance with the RAF's exacting standards.

Sqn Ldr Neville Duke (centre) welcomes his old aeroplanes back to Tangmere. Having flown WB188 to achieve the air speed record in September 1953, and more recently having become Honorary President of Tangmere Museum, it was gratifying for him to see both the Hunter and Meteor back at Tangmere. Although he had not flown Meteor EE549 on its record-breaking flight he had been part of the 1946 High Speed Flight and had flown the aeroplane several times. In this picture he is flanked by museum directors Peter Dimond (left) and Andy Saunders, author of this book.

Removing the wings and centre section of EE549 from its flatbed truck inside the museum was problematical owing to limited headroom for the two cranes. Plenty of careful easing and nudging of the load finally achieved the desired result – and the museum roof remained intact! The re-assembly by a team of RAF technicians and civilians was completed in just a couple of days and without a scratch to either aeroplane.

The cockpit section of EE549 is rejoined to the fuselage as the operation draws to a successful conclusion. The high-gloss, high-speed finish of the Meteor is clearly evident in this photograph. Through the open doors of the display hall can be seen a T-33 Shooting Star, acquired on loan by the author from the USAF in 1977 and held in open storage until the opening of the museum in 1982.

The aviation equivalent of a topping-out ceremony as the fin of Hunter WB188 is slotted into position, thus completing this epic operation. The prestige of acquiring and displaying these aeroplanes was richly deserved for a place so famous in RAF history as Tangmere, not least because of their associations with the place.

The end of the story! Two immaculate aeroplanes in their immaculate new 'hangar' at Tangmere Museum where they are now viewed by thousands of visitors each year. They epitomize the achievements of all who served at RAF Tangmere between 1918 and 1970, and of those who created the museum.

RAF TANGMERE STATION COMMANDERS

Maj W.V. Strugnell MC	March 1918
Flt Lt H.L. Nunn DSC, DFC	June 1925
Flt Lt T.G. Bowler	April 1926
Wg Cdr J.H.S. Tyssen MC	November 1926
Sqn Ldr E.O. Grenfell MC, DFC, AFC	October 1928
Wg Cdr J.B. Graham MC, AFC	December 1928
Wg Cdr R.M. Drummond OBE, DSO, MC	November 1931
Wg Cdr G.C. Pirie MC, DFC	June 1933
Wg Cdr E.G. Hopcraft DSC	August 1934
Wg Cdr R.B. Mansell OBE	February 1935
Wg Cdr L.H. Slatter OBE, DSC, DFC	August 1935
Wg Cdr C.W. Hill	April 1937
Gp Capt. K.R. Park MC, DFC, ADC	December 1937
Gp Capt. F. Sowrey DSO, MC, AFC	June 1938
Gp Capt. C.H. Nicholas DFC, AFC	August 1939
Wg Cdr I.A. Bertram	October 1939
Wg Cdr C.L. Lea-Cox	February 1940
Gp Capt. J.A. Boret OBE, ME, AFC	July 1940
Gp Capt. A.B. Woodall OBE	April 1941
Gp Capt. C.H. Appleton DSO, DFC	January 1942
Gp Capt. H.D. McGregor DSO	September 1942
Gp Capt. W.J. Crisham	May 1943
Wg Cdr P.R. Walker DSO, DFC	February 1944
Wg Cdr N.J. Starr DFC	September 1944
Gp Capt. D.M. Somerville	October 1944
Wg Cdr J.A. O'Neill DFC	November 1944
Air Cdre R.L.R. Atcherley OBE, AFC	January 1945
Air Cdre G.D. Harvey	September 1945
Wg Cdr R.J. Hardiman DFC	October 1945
Wg Cdr C.H. Dyson MBE, DFC	May 1946
Wg Cdr W.G. Clouston DFC	June 1946
Wg Cdr G.S.A. Parnaby OBE	September 1947
Gp Capt. T.O. Prickett DSO, DFC	August 1949
Gp Capt. S.C. Elworthy CBE, DSO, DFC, AFC	December 1951
Gp Capt. J.A. Kent DFC, AFC	March 1953
Gp Capt. E.A. Whiteley CBE, DFC	November 1955
Gp Capt. R.I.K. Edwards DFC, AFC	April 1956
Wg Cdr H.E. Walmsley DFC	June 1958
Wg Cdr W.W.T. Ritchie OBE, AFC	August 1958
Gp Capt. W.D. David CBE, DFC, AFC	September 1958
Gp Capt. P.A. Hughes DFC	May 1961
Wg Cdr E.R. Dutt AFC	October 1963
Wg Cdr P.D.J. Wood DFC	February 1965
Wg Cdr D. Gray AFC	April 1968

Acknowledgements

I would like to thank all those who have helped with photographs and information collected over many years. I have endeavoured to mention everyone and apologize for any unintentional omissions:

Wing Commander H.R. Allen • P. Arnold • Group Captain D. Bader • J. Beedle
Air Vice Marshall H.A.C. Bird-Wilson • British Rail • P. Burgess • *Chichester Observer*
P. Cole • G. Craig • T. Davies • P. Dimond • D. Dunstall • Squadron Leader N. Duke
B. Field • *Flight* • Fox Photos • N. Franks • R. Freeman • R. Gilbert • G. Hazell
J. Hickman • Imperial War Museum • Ministry of Defence • F. Prebble • RAF Museum
W.G. Ramsay • D. Sarkar • D. Tozer • *Topix* • Group Captain H. Verity • M. Zebedee

In addition I owe special thanks to Zoë Broome for her help in preparing the layout.

BRITAIN IN OLD PHOTOGRAPHS

SUTTON'S PHOTOGRAPHIC HISTORY OF TRANSPORT

To order any of these titles please telephone our distributor, Littlehampton Book Services on 01903 828800
For a catalogue of these and our other titles please ring Emma Leitch on 01453 731114